KV-118-300

Deserts

Patricia Monahan

Macdonald Educational

Contents

How to use this book

This book tells you about deserts. Although there are both hot and cold deserts in the world we will look mainly at the hot deserts. Look first at the contents page to see if the subject you are looking for is listed. For instance if you want to find out about irrigation, you will see that this is found on page 32. The index will tell you where and how many times a particular subject is mentioned and whether there is a picture of it. Troglodytes, for example, you will find on pages 38-39. The glossary explains the more difficult terms found in this book.

What is a desert?

The deserts of the world cover about a quarter of the land surface of the Earth. Although they cover quite a large area only 5% of the Earth's population live in them. What makes a desert so difficult to live in?

Characteristics

Deserts have a very small amount of rain each year, less than 25 cm. The rain does not fall evenly, but falls occasionally in violent storms. There are sometimes many years between the storms. Although many deserts have very high temperatures, there are cold deserts too. They are found thousands of metres above sea level and near the poles. Even cold deserts do not have enough water, as most of it is permanently frozen in the soil. Plants and animals cannot use it.

Most deserts have very few plants and a very thin layer of soil. The soil and rocks are constantly changed by the wind and the little water that there is. Life in the desert is a very hard struggle.

Contrasts

Deserts are areas of very great contrasts. Hot deserts are very hot in the day and very cold at night. They have long periods of drought and violent storms. They can be found high in the mountains and on low-lying plains. They can be areas of bare rock, or covered with sand. The plants and animals that live in deserts have to adapt themselves in many ways to live in these hot, dry lands.

Many kinds of people live in the deserts of the world. They vary from the primitive bushmen who just scrape a living from the desert to the rich oil sheiks who live in wealth and splendour. Many great civilizations have grown and fallen in desert lands, while the life of the Australian aborigine has remained unchanged for thousands of years.

Changes

Life in the desert is changing slowly. As the population of the world grows it becomes more important to use as much land as we can. Modern scientific developments are helping us to do this, as we learn more about the plants and animals that live in the desert.

People, plants and animals have all learnt to live in the desert.

6

Large saguaro cacti are common in the desert area of North America.

Where are the deserts?

Although the deserts of the world have much in common, they have many differences too. They can be hot or cold, rocky or sandy, some are very large and some are small. Some have quite large numbers of people living on them, others are so barren that it is difficult for plants, animals and people to survive.

The deserts of North America have far more plants

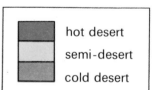

▨	hot desert
☐	semi-desert
▨	cold desert

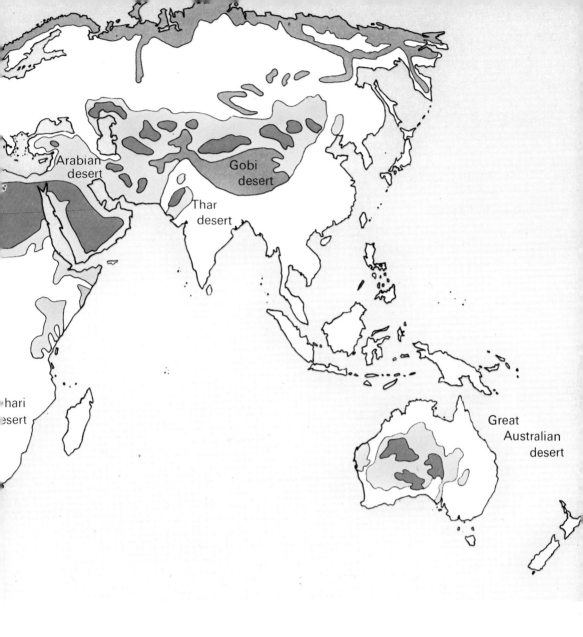

Arabian
desert

Gobi
desert

Thar
desert

hari
esert

Great
Australian
desert

Deserts are spread throughout the world from the cold deserts of the north to those at the tip of South America. Many thousands of years ago a world map showing deserts would have looked very different from this one. No doubt in the future the map will continue to change.

than the others. It is there that the very large cacti grow. Some deserts are often covered by fog. Others are cloudless. Some deserts are rich in minerals while others are not.

Deserts are to be found all over the world. They are not all areas of great heat. The word 'desert' in fact comes from 'deserted place'. They are places where no one lives. The areas near the Poles and high in the mountains of central Asia are as much deserts as the Sahara.

9

How are deserts made?

There are four main ways in which a desert can be made. Deserts are always formed because there is not enough water. The reasons for the shortage of rain are different.

Equatorial deserts

There are two bands of deserts along the equator. The direction of the wind has helped to form these deserts. If you look at the diagram of planetary winds you will see that there are some places that have high pressure. If this happens it means that the air is very calm and there is very little wind. If there is no wind the clouds carrying rain are not brought to the desert areas. The Sahara, Arabian, Central Australian, Kalahari and Atacama deserts are all affected by high pressure.

Continental deserts

Arid, or dry regions, are also caused by areas being very far from the sea. Winds pick up moisture when they are blowing over the sea. When they reach land this moisture falls as rain. By the time winds

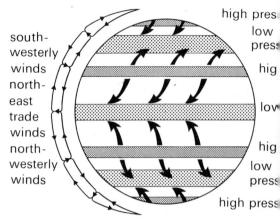

south-westerly winds

north-east trade winds

north-westerly winds

high pres
low press
hig
low
hig
low
press
high press

Above: Just as the waters of the oceans move around in currents so the air has patterns of movement. These air movements are the winds. There are two sorts of winds. There are the local ones that may change from day to day or week to week. Then there are the planetary winds. The planetary winds blow in the same direction all the time. In the northern hemisphere they are bent to the right by the rotation of the Earth. In the southern hemisphere the opposite happens.

Below: Areas in the middle of continents are sometimes deserts as the wind has travelled so far over dry land that it does not carry any rain with it. The shaded areas show this sort of desert.

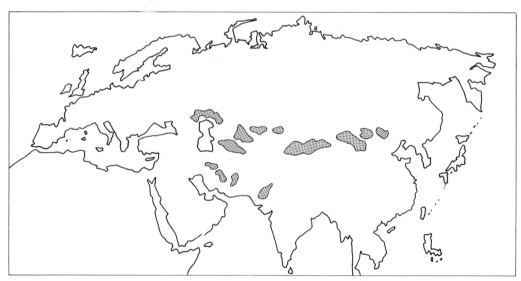

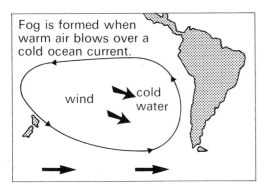

Fog is formed when warm air blows over a cold ocean current.

wind

cold water

Above: In South America a cold ocean current runs up the west coast. The winds blowing across this cold current are carrying moisture. When they come in contact with the cold water the moisture that they carry merges into larger drops and forms fog. Coastal deserts often have a lot of fog, but very little rain.

Below: Clouds carrying moisture rise when they come to hills or mountains. As they rise they come in contact with colder air which makes raindrops form. When the drops are too large to be held in the air they fall as rain. The side of the mountain away from the wind does not have nearly so much rain as the clouds have let it fall before they reach here. Sometimes deserts are formed.

have reached far inland they have already shed most of their water and there is no more to fall. So some inland areas are deserts.

Rain shadow deserts

Sometimes mountains prevent rain from reaching deserts. The monsoon winds that cross the Indian Ocean drop their rain when they rise to blow over mountains called the Western Ghats. The Deccan, the area behind the mountains, is very dry. In North and South America the Rockies and the Andes mountains also help to create desert regions.

Coastal deserts

Along the coasts of South America and South Africa are the Atacama and Namib deserts which are very arid regions. Cold currents from the Antarctic run along these coasts. The winds that travel over these currents are cool and cannot carry much moisture. The air is sometimes moist enough to form fog and these coastal deserts have many foggy days.

Most deserts are not formed because of just one of these reasons. It is usually because of several of them.

Desert climates

Although all deserts have one thing in common, a very low rainfall, they can look very different indeed. Even within one desert there can be great changes. The Hoggar mountains in the middle of the Sahara have slightly more rain than the surrounding land. As a result more plants and animals live there.

Daily changes

In most deserts it is very hot during the day. At night, as there are no clouds, the heat escapes from the land very quickly. It can be bitterly cold.

Historical changes

During the last 1000 million years the climate on Earth has changed several times. During the Ice Ages the ice sheets extended over a much wider area than they do now. At other times the climate became much hotter and more tropical. Then the polar regions would not have been covered with ice and snow. Areas which are deserts now once had plenty of water. Places with plenty of rain today were once deserts.

Finding the changes

Scientists think that in earlier times large lakes existed in areas that are now deserts. Experts can find soil and rocks that would only have been on the bottom of a lake or along its shores. They have proved that Lake Bonneville in the USA was once a very large lake covering 30,000 square kilometres. Today all that remains of this vast lake is the Great Salt Lake which covers only 3,000 square kilometres.

Lake Chad in the southern Sahara has shrunk within the memories of some of the people who live there now. Recently

These rock paintings done thousands of years ago show that cows must have lived in areas that are now deserts.

the fringes of the Sahara have also been suffering from drought. The desert is beginning to take over areas that are now used for grazing.

In Melbourne fossilized sand dunes have been found. This is evidence that many years ago the area must have been a desert.

Rhinos in the desert

The Tassili N'Ajjer is a plateau 2,100 metres high in the south east of Algeria. The ground is parched and cracked and there are few plants. However, archaeologists have found many things that show the area must once have had a large population.

In 1937 a man called Lieutenant Brenans discovered rock paintings and carvings showing animals like elephants, giraffes, rhinoceros and fish. There were even pictures of pools of water. At one time these animals must have lived in what are now desert regions. Scientists have also found the remains of a domestic cow which are about 20,000 years old.

Rainfall

All deserts are dry places and because of this the small amount of rain that does fall becomes very important. Quite small differences in the amount of rain or the number of storms can cause very great differences in the sort of plant, animal and human life of the desert.

Winds

In many desert regions there are seasonal winds that are hot, dry and dusty. They make life very uncomfortable. These winds blow from the centre of the desert. They have local names. In the southern Sahara the wind is called the Harmattan, in the north the Khamsin. In the Mediterranean area there is the Sirocco.

A mirage is caused by a heat haze. It looks as though there is a large pool of water in the desert. The trees are reflected in the 'water'.

The work of water

Although water is very scarce in deserts, it has played a large part in the way they look. One of the hazards of camping in the desert is drowning! The dry river beds called *wadis* can flood in minutes without warning. The bones of animals that have been caught by these flash floods are found all along the wadis. In some parts of the Sahara *quicksands* are another unexpected hazard.

Desert rainfall

There are several reasons why the water which falls in dry regions has such an important part to play in shaping the landscape. The rain falls in short violent storms. Although these may be several years apart their effect is much greater than the more evenly distributed rainfall of European countries.

As there is so little plant cover the soil and rocks are exposed to the full force of the rain. There is also nothing to bind the rocks and soil together so the top layers are washed away. When more rain falls the process begins again. The loose material is picked up by the water as it runs off and as it falls on the rocks it helps to break them down too.

Water does not sink down into the ground. There are no plants to trap it on the surface. In desert areas a hard mineral crust forms over the surface of the ground.

The water works on the desert landscape over many thousands of years. The best example of the effect that water has had on an arid landscape is the North American desert. However, all desert landscapes are shaped not only by water, but by wind too.

mountains

Above: Ayers rock in Australia rises dramatically in the flat, dry land surrounding it.

The characteristics of the American desert are very distinct. Water and wind have shaped the landscape.

mesas

butte

alt pan

vial fans

Seif dunes

Barchan dunes

Star dunes

The shape of sand dunes
depends on the direction
of the wind.

The work of wind

The wind acts on the desert landscape in three different ways. It helps to erode, or wear away, the land, it carries away the eroded materials and it deposits them somewhere else.

Erosion

Sand is made of tiny particles of a very hard material called *quartz*. The sand is picked up by the wind and thrown against rock surfaces. Gradually, over millions of years, the softer parts of the rock are worn away. Sometimes, even the harder parts of rock are so undercut that they break off too. The wind sculpts the rocks into fantastic shapes. The great American desert has the most varied and splendid rock sculptures, spires and bridges.

Transport

The wind has another, less spectacular effect, on deserts. These are desert depressions. They are caused by *deflation*—a process where the wind carries away the very smallest particles of sand but leaves the rest behind. The desert depression has a surface which looks like a pavement. Larger stones are set in finer particles of sand. These areas are called *gibber plains* in Australia and *hammada* in North Africa.

Deposition

Once the wind has eroded and transported material it has to put it down somewhere else. This is called *deposition*. A very important product of the desert wind is *loess*. Loess is a deposit of very fine soil. It can be found on the edges of the arid areas in Asia, in central Europe and in central USA. It is extremely fertile and is usually planted with food crops.

Sand dunes

Most people probably think that sand dunes are the most typical scenery of desert regions. However, only about a third of the desert regions of the world have sand dunes. In the American desert only a tenth of the total area is covered by sand dunes.

The particles of sand are carried along by the wind and piled into heaps which gradually increase in size. The different shapes depend on wind direction.

Although all desert landscapes are harsh and dry, they can look very different. The top picture shows shifting sand dunes.

The two bottom photographs show the different sorts of rocky deserts: one flat with small stones and the other with rugged hills and valleys.

moose

caribou

wolf

The moose and caribou travel south in the winter to find plants to eat. The wolf stays in the tundra.

Cold deserts

Cold deserts are found in two different sorts of places. They are found at high altitudes and near the North and South Poles. The cold deserts near the North Pole are usually called *tundra*.

Characteristics

The cold deserts near the poles have low temperatures, low rainfall and short summers. The ground is generally covered with snow. The ground more than three metres down is permanently frozen. This is called the *permafrost*.

During the summer when the snow on the surface begins to thaw, this layer of frozen ground acts as a barrier to the melting water. Large quantities of water collect on the surface of the ground. As there is suddenly plenty of water the plants, such as lichens, mosses and flowers, grow very quickly.

In the summer there is continual daylight and during the winter there is continual darkness. These areas do not have days and nights as we know them.

Plant life

Most plants in the tundra are *perennial*. This means that they live for several years, dying down in the winter and growing again the following summer. In regions where the growing season is very short it is important that plants are ready to grow and fruit as soon as conditions are suitable.

Animals in the tundra

Some animals, like the polar bear, wolf, fox and weasel, live in the tundra all the time. Other animals like the musk ox and the caribou, migrate. They travel north in the summer and return to warmer places in the south when winter comes.

Birds too are divided into those that migrate and those that live in the tundra all the time. Geese and ducks travel backwards and forward as the seasons change. The snowy owl and the ptarmigan adapt themselves to the harsh conditions all the year round.

People

Eskimos learnt to live in the tundra by adapting to the harsh conditions around them. They were excellent hunters. Seal and fish were a very important part of their diet. In the summer they also ate berries, which they gathered, and small mammals. They made their clothes from the fur of the animals they killed. The furry side was always next to the skin. It trapped a layer of warm air which helped to keep the Eskimos warm.

The caribou was especially important to Eskimos. They used its hide to make their summer tents and for clothing and bags. Its meat, blood and organs were eaten by the Eskimos themselves, or fed to their dogs. Its bones, antlers, teeth and

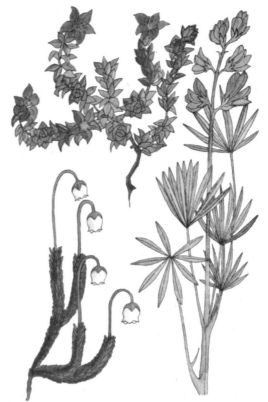

Above: Flowers in the tundra bloom when the snow melts in the summer and provides water for the plants.

hooves were made into bows, arrow points, tools, games, jewellery, combs, snow goggles and needle cases. Its sinew was used as thread.

However, fewer and fewer of the Eskimos live in the old way. The ancient skills are dying out.

In the summer when the ground thaws the plants grow and mature very quickly.

Vegetation

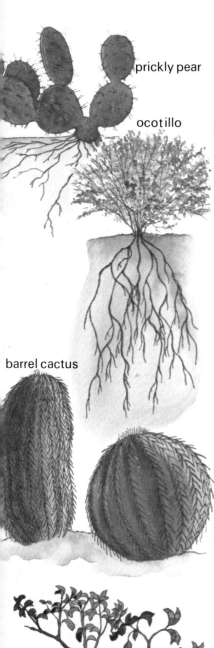

prickly pear

ocotillo

barrel cactus

tamarisk

Plants need water for several reasons. Plant tissue is 90% water. They need water to carry minerals from the ground, through the root system and to all the parts of the plant. It is also needed for *photosynthesis*. Photosynthesis is the process that plants use to convert energy from the sun and carbon dioxide from the air into food. Water also controls the temperature of the plant, which is very important in the desert. Plants have learnt to live in the desert by adapting themselves to the arid conditions and living without much water.

The drought resisters

Plants in the desert have learnt to survive by making the best possible use of every drop of water. Many plants have hairy or waxy leaves which help to stop the plant losing water from the leaf surface. The acacia can shed or curl its leaves to reduce water loss when conditions get very bad.

The plant that most people think of when they think of the desert is the cactus. Cacti are called *succulents* because they can store water in their tissues. The barrel cactus stores water in its stem. As the water is used up the plant shrinks. Cacti come in all shapes and sizes from very tiny plants to those which are much taller than people.

Some plants like the tamarisk and the eucalyptus have developed very large root systems to use water stored deep under ground. The baobab tree which grows on the edge of the desert has survived because of its large swollen trunk. It stores water in its trunk.

The escapers

Some desert plants are *annuals*. This means that a new plant grows each year from seeds left behind from previous years. Sometimes the seeds have to wait for years until conditions are right for them to grow. As soon as there is rain and enough moisture for them to grow they burst into bloom. They produce seeds and die. When annuals bloom the desert is carpeted with colour, but these plants only live for a very short time and the colour soon fades.

Above left : Yucca in the New Mexico desert.
Above right : Cacti often have very brightly coloured flowers.

Below : After rainfall the desert is covered in flowers. These ones are desert dandelions.

Invertebrates

Invertebrates are animals that do not have a backbone. They are animals like spiders, insects and molluscs. These animals can be found in all the deserts of the world.

Animals in the desert face two problems. First of all they have to learn to save as much water as possible. Normal body functions such as breathing and excreting waste materials use water. The second problem is to keep their bodies at a reasonable temperature in such an extreme climate.

Small animals have an extra problem. They have a large surface area compared to their body size. As water loss can take place all over the surface of their body this is a problem that has to be solved. Insects have solved it by having a waterproof covering called an *integument* on their bodies.

Desert life styles

Snails have learnt to live in the desert by hiding away in the heat of the day. They only come out to look for food in the cooler periods. They mate directly after a rainfall. The ferocious ant lion protects its larvae from the heat of the desert by building a cone-shaped pit. The larvae live in this and catch and eat other insects that go past.

Some crickets have developed hairy legs which help them to travel more easily over the desert sand. Many burrowing insects have short legs that are particularly suited to digging. The desert locust survives because it is able to travel great distances in search of food and water.

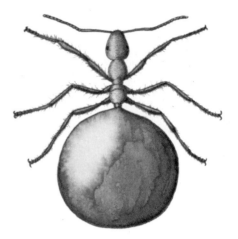

honeydew ant

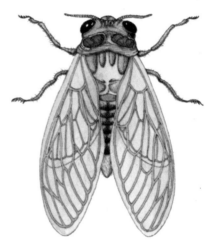

cicada

scorpion

anise swallowtail

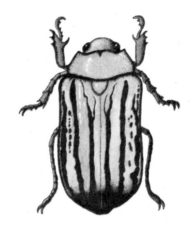

scarab beetle

tarantula hawk killing a tarantula

hunting wasp

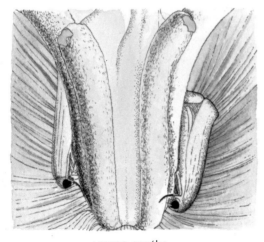

yucca moths

wolf spider

Above: Gila woodpeckers peck holes in saguaro cacti to use as nests.

Below: This elf owl has taken over a nesting hole made by a gila woodpecker.

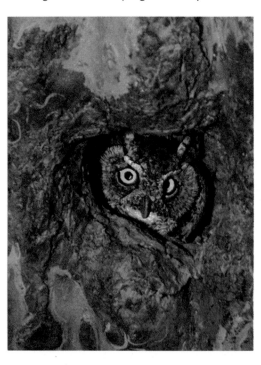

Birds

Unlike other animals that live in the desert, birds have made very little change in either shape or colour to help them to survive. However, the birds are usually paler in colour than those in other places.

Unless the birds eat the succulents that grow in the desert they must drink water every day. They have to live near drinking water.

Birds that eat insects and meat get most of the water they need from their food. Birds that eat seeds that do not contain so much moisture economize on water by producing small amounts of very concentrated urine.

Keeping cool

Birds cannot put up with great heat. As most birds are active during the day they must find some sort of cover for themselves. There are many birds in the deserts of North America. The cacti and shrubby trees provide plenty of cover. The thorns of the cacti keep off any predators that might attack the birds.

The burrowing owl hunts for its food at night-time. In the daytime it avoids the heat by hiding in an abandoned burrow of a ground squirrel.

The sand grouse has special feathers on the underside of its body which can absorb water. The bird uses these feathers to moisten its eggs and prevent them from becoming too hot.

The ostrich has a special problem. It is so large that it cannot find shelter as the smaller birds do. It needs large amounts of water to survive. It has special glands in its nose which allow it to live off salty water as well as fresh water.

roadrunner

emu

rhea

Temminck's
horned lark

peregrine falcon

esert lark

ostrich

vulture

sand grouse

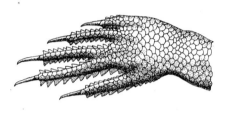

Reptiles and amphibian

More reptiles are found in desert regions than *amphibians*. Amphibians need water to breed in. So they can only live in desert areas that are quite close to water.

Lizards

One very common desert reptile is the lizard. Lizards feed mostly on insects and plants. Some of the larger ones eat small animals. Some lizards look very fierce. When the chuckwalla lizard is threatened it runs into a crevice. Then it blows itself up like a balloon. Its enemy cannot possibly pull it out of the hole, it is wedged in so tightly.

Some lizards have valves in their noses to prevent sand blowing into them and also prevent moisture from escaping. Their heads are wedge-shaped to help them move through the sand easily. Scales on their toes help them to move through and over the sand.

Snakes

Snakes cannot survive in very high temperatures. However, they can usually squeeze themselves into very small nooks and crannies. They manage to avoid the hot parts of the day like this. They get most of the water they need from the flesh of the animals they eat.

Toads

Not many amphibians live in the desert. However, there are a few sorts of toad which manage to survive by burying themselves in the ground during very dry periods. Sometimes they live like this for several months. They come out to mate when the rain falls and lay their eggs in pools of water. The eggs hatch and the toads grow in a very short time.

Above: Lizards' feet have adapted to the problems of travelling on and through sand.

Below: The gecko can protect its eyes by nearly covering them with a thin layer of skin.

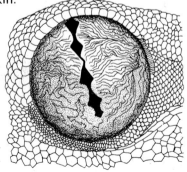

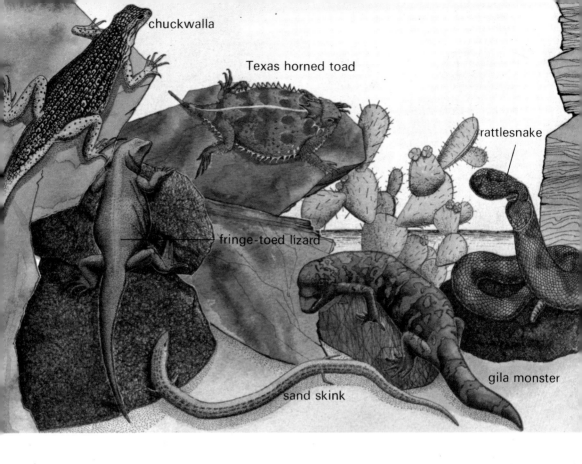

chuckwalla

Texas horned toad

rattlesnake

fringe-toed lizard

gila monster

sand skink

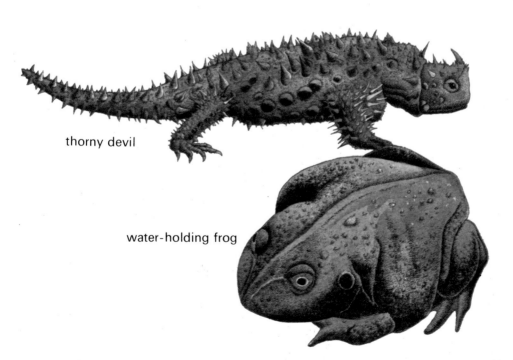

thorny devil

water-holding frog

Desert mammals

Many small mammals called *rodents* live in the desert. One of them, the kangaroo rat, burrows into the ground to avoid the midday sun. It has short front legs to help it burrow. It comes out at night time to look for food. It is then much cooler. Kangaroo rats always have to be on the alert for animals like foxes and owls who will kill them for food. The rats have long back legs that help them to escape very quickly. They drink almost no water, they have to get the moisture they need from the food they eat.

If the kangaroo rat is attacked by a rattlesnake it escapes by kicking sand in its eyes. The snake is blinded for long enough to allow the rat to escape. But this method does not protect it from all its enemies.

Many of the mammals that live in desert regions have to travel large distances to find food. The larger mammals particularly must search hard for enough food and water to survive. Unlike the small mammals they cannot hide from the heat of the sun by burrowing under ground. Very few animals live in the very dry desert centres. They usually live on the fringes where conditions are not quite so harsh.

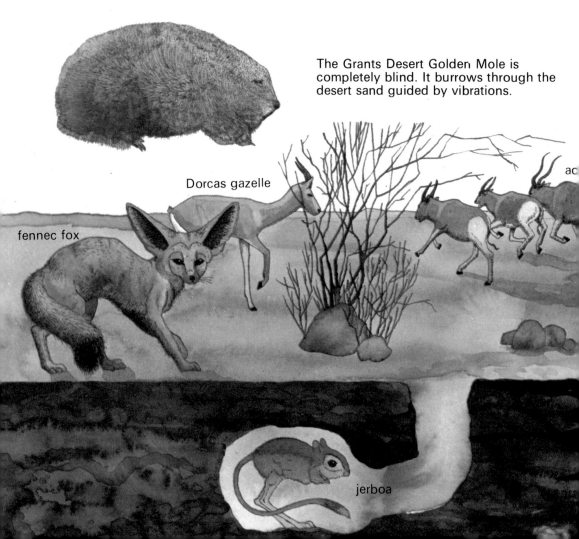

The Grants Desert Golden Mole is completely blind. It burrows through the desert sand guided by vibrations.

ad

Dorcas gazelle

fennec fox

jerboa

kangaroos

numbat

kangaroo rat

rt
ehog

The carnivores

Many meat eating animals live on the fringes of desert areas. They include foxes, jackals, hyaenas, small cats and the Australian dingo. The only one to live in really arid conditions is the fennec fox which lives in the Sahara. It also has a close relative, the kit fox, which lives in the North American desert. The fennec fox hunts at night time, living mainly on small rodents. It has large ears to help it hear the rats moving around. It also has very sharp eyes.

The larger mammals

Some large mammals live in the desert too. There are hoofed animals like antelopes, gazelles and wild asses. In Australia there are the pouched or *marsupial* mammals like the kangaroos and wallabies. In North America there are pronghorns and muledeer. All of these animals are able to live with only very small amounts of water. Sometimes they travel very long distances to find water. Nearly all of them are *herbivores* which means that they only eat grass and plants.

Domestic animals

People who live in the desert areas of the world depend on animals for several things. They need them for food, for hides and for transport.

Camels

There are two types of camel. The Arabian camel or dromedary which has only one hump and the bactrian camel which has two humps. The bactrian is sturdier than the dromedary and has a thicker coat of hair. The bactrian camel lives in the mountains of central Asia where the winters are very cold.

The camel is used mainly for transport. It can easily carry a load of more than 200 kilos. It can travel for many days carrying heavy loads as long as it is allowed to rest sometimes. Camels are not bothered by heat or cold. To help them survive in the deserts they can drink vast quantities of water at one time. They can drink as much as 120 litres and then survive several days without more water.

Camels' feet are specially adapted to help them travel easily across the sand. They have pads on them which act like snowshoes and stop the camel sinking into the soft sand. Camels have long eyelashes to stop sand getting in their eyes. They can close their nostrils to stop the sand blowing in their noses.

Other animals

The Mongols who live high up in the Pamir mountains keep herds of yak. The yak is a relative of the domestic cow. It is very hardy.

The Indians of the Atacama desert in South America keep llamas. The llama is related to the camel. Like the camel the llama is used for transport, but its flesh is also eaten and its wool makes very good cloth.

Nearly all the people who live in desert areas keep sheep and goats. In some areas Zebu cattle are kept. They have humps on their backs which store fat. When food is in short supply they can live on the stored fat.

A great deal of money is being spent to carry out research on breeds of animals that can live in desert conditions.

Bactrian camel

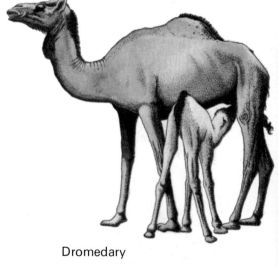
Dromedary

Above: Herds of sheep must travel over a wide area to find grass to graze. Grass grows very thinly in desert areas.

Below: Berbers breed horses to race in fast, exciting games.

Below: Cattle are the main product of the large ranches in Texas.

Above: Many types of water wheels are used for irrigation. This one is in Morocco.
Below: This long straight canal has been built for irrigation in Hasa oasis, Saudi Arabia.

Irrigation

Irrigation is artificially watering land so that plants can grow. Watering the garden with a hose or sprinkler is a sort of irrigation. People have been using different methods of irrigation for thousands of years. Ancient Egyptian paintings and sculptures show the types of irrigation that were used 4,000 years ago.

Three of the world's most important ancient civilizations grew up because the people learnt how to use river water to irrigate the desert lands they lived in. They developed many technical skills and built quite complicated systems. They built dams, drainage systems and equipment for lifting and carrying water. They looked after the irrigation systems very carefully because all their crops depended on them. Some of these methods were so complex that people, even today, have not built such good irrigation systems.

Herodotus, a historian who lived in the fifth century BC described Egypt as 'a land won by the Egyptians and given them by the river'. The river he was talking about is the Nile. The Egyptians still depend on it today for irrigating their crops.

Mesopotamia

The word 'Mesopotamia' comes from the Greek and means 'between two rivers'. The rivers that this civilization grew up on were the Tigris and the Euphrates. The area is surrounded by desert and the people were completely dependent on the rivers for survival. The civilization reached its height about 2500 BC and many important cities were built.

The Indus

The third of the civilizations existed between 2500 and 1600 BC. It grew up by the Indus River which starts in Tibet and flows south to the Arabian Sea.

The Nabateans

There are other types of irrigation besides those using rivers. The Nabateans live in the highlands of the Negev desert. They survived because they learnt how to make the most use of the little rainfall that they had. They collected it and used it to water their fields in the valleys in times of drought.

Quanats

Quanats are systems for using underground water. The water is channelled through tunnels. They were first used in ancient Iran. Then they were used in many desert areas and are still in use today.

Mechanical aids

Many very simple mechanical tools are still used in arid areas, just as they have been for thousands of years. The *shaduf* is a very simple device. It is made of a pole supported on a cross bar. There is a bucket on one end and a weight on the other end to balance it. The bucket is pulled into the well with a rope and when it is full the weight lifts it up again.

The *sakia*, or Persian wheel, is a wheel with a continuous chain of buckets. It is turned by an ox. While one set of buckets is being filled, the other is being emptied.

Another method of carrying water is by using the *Archimedes screw*. This is a mechanism which works just like an ordinary screw and carries the water upwards.

Filling water bottles in Nigeria. Water sometimes has to be carried long distances from the well.

Hunters and gatherers

Although deserts cover very large areas very few of the world's people live in them. But people do manage to overcome these difficult conditions. The simplest way of life is that of hunting and gathering The last surviving people to live in this primitive way are the Bushmen of the Kalahari desert in Botswana and the Australian aborigines.

The Bushmen

The Bushmen travel round their territory in small groups made up of several families. They travel around in search of game. The men are very good marksmen and can hit a moving antelope at 130 metres. They do not have modern fire-arms. Any large animals that they kill are first wounded with a poisoned arrow and then they are trailed, sometimes for long distances. Finally the animal is killed with a spear.

The part of the animal where the spear entered is eaten on the spot. This is an ancient custom which the hunters still follow. The rest is taken back to the camp. Any meat which is not eaten straight away is cut into strips and dried. The dried meat is called biltong. It can be kept for quite a long time without going bad.

When the hunters cannot find any game they eat roots. The women collect the roots.

Water is always a problem. The bush-

The Bushmen of the Kalahari desert build themselves very primitive shelters.

men are very skilled at finding and saving what little water there is around. Even a patch of damp sand can give them a few drops of water. Water is sucked up through a reed. A bundle of grass is used as a filter. This is called a sip well. The water collected is stored in gourds and ostrich eggs. Sometimes the water is buried for use in droughts.

The Bushmen sleep naked in the open although it gets very cold at night. Their only shelter is a windbreak made of twigs and grass. It helps to reflect the heat of their fire.

The territory of the Bushmen once covered a much larger area of southern Africa than it does now.

The Bindibu

Most of the Australian aborigines have abandoned their traditional way of life. Only the Bindibu still live as their ancestors did thousands of years ago. The Bindibu have no crops, no clothes, no homes, no utensils. Like the Bushmen they sleep in the open with only a small fire for warmth.

The Bindibu travel in small groups following the small amounts of rain that fall. When they do find a pool of water they usually kneel down on all fours to drink. They do not have any drinking or water storing utensils. They also get water from the sap of plants and trees.

If the huntsmen have been successful they eat emu or kangaroo meat, otherwise they eat grubs, insects and roots collected by the women.

Australian aborigines hunting kangaroos with boomerangs, their traditional weapons.

Herders

The best use of desert lands that people can make is to keep animals on it. People who herd animals in the desert are constantly moving around to find new pastures and water. They are called nomads.

The Bedouin

'Bedouin' means 'desert dwellers'. The Bedouins have lived in the deserts of Arabia and North Africa for over 2,000 years.

The Bedouins live in tents woven from goats' hair. The tents are simple to put up and take down. This is very important as the Bedouin are always moving to find

The Bedouin women do much of their work outside their tents. The children, from a very early age, are expected to help their parents. The girls help their mother and the boys their father.

new pastures and water for their animals. They sometimes only stay for one day at a camp site.

The tents the Bedouins live in are divided into two sections. In the front one the men will entertain visitors with tea or coffee and talk about the affairs of the tribe. The back section of the tent is used by the women and children. The food is prepared in the back part and the family sleep here too.

Both the men and women wear loose fitting clothes with several layers. These provide good insulation and keep them cool during the day and warm at night. The men wear a head veil which is held in place by a band of rope. The veil protects the head and neck from the sun. It can also be held across the face to keep out dust and sand. The women are required to keep their faces covered with a veil when they are with strangers.

Food made from milk and bread are the main diet of the Bedouin. For special occasions a sheep or goat is killed.

The Bedouin are gradually moving away from their nomadic way of life to settle in villages. Here they cultivate the land. Some of them find work in the cities or on oilfields.

The Tuareg

The Tuareg are nomadic people who live in the Air, Hoggar and Tassili N'Ajjer mountains of the Sahara. They are tall, handsome people. It is not known where they come from. Their skins are much lighter than most of the people who live in the Sahara. Although they follow the same religion as other Arabs they have different laws and customs. Women play a more important part in society than is usual with Arabs. They do not cover their faces. In their society it is the men who must cover their head and faces.

They wear a long length of light cotton that is arranged in a special way. It is called a tanguelmoust.

The Tuareg were once the pirates of the desert. They raided the oases and slave caravans and were always involved in feuds and wars. Now, however, they are just struggling to survive in the harsh conditions of the desert.

The Mongols

The Mongols live in the arid regions of central Asia. They live high up in the Gobi desert. They herd sheep, goats and yaks. Their tents are called yurts. They make them from fur and hide. They are built in a round shape and the thick walls protect the Mongols from the cold winds of the Gobi desert.

Here Bedouin women are weaving using a very simple loom. Many of the brightly coloured blankets and rugs they will have made themselves. Nomadic people have to be very independent.

Oasis dwellers

An oasis is a fertile area in a desert. It may develop around a natural supply of water like a river or spring or it may be man-made and be created in mining or oil-drilling areas. Where there is no natural supply of water nearby it may have to be brought from great distances by pipelines or in tankers.

Oases are different from other settlements. They are totally isolated like an island. The people who live there must provide as much as they can for themselves. Other goods which they need have to be brought from far away. As the people are so isolated they are cut off from other ways of life so their own lives go on unchanged for hundreds of years.

The palm tree

There is a story that when Allah created people he found that he had two lumps of clay left over. With one he made a camel, with the other he made a palm tree. Both of these things are very important to people who live in the desert. Now people are beginning to use mechanized transport instead of camels, but nothing has replaced the palm tree. The dates which grow on these trees are very nutritious and are part of the diet of most oasis dwellers for about six months of the year. Dates keep very well and even the stones are used. They are a tasty treat for the camels. The sap of the tree is used to make palm wine. The trunks are used for fuel. Fibre is used for rope, net, sacks and raffia. The leaves are used for bedding and to make shelters. The tall date palms also provide shelter for the other crops that are grown in oases.

Above: Navaho dwellings in a cave mouth.

Below: Troglodyte dwellings in Tunisia. The white houses on the ground were built by the government, but few people wanted to live in them.

Mozabites

The Mozabites are a group of people who went to live in the Sahara to escape religious persecution. They settled in a series of walled towns called Ghardaia. They were built along the River M'zab which is dry for most of the year. To get water they have built wells and irrigation channels. They grow oranges, dates and vegetables in groves outside the city walls. They are a trading people. The men often spend several years at a time away from home.

Troglodytes

Troglodytes are people who live in caves. There is a group of troglodytes who live in northern Tunisia. They make their homes in cave-like rooms under the ground. The dwellings are very practical They are cool in summer and warm in winter. The people refused to move when the government wanted to give them ordinary houses.

Ranching

The homesteads of the cattle ranchers of the United States and the sheep farmers of Australia are really other examples of oasis dwellings. At first these settlements might not seem to be oases, but they have much in common with traditional oases. They are isolated, they must have a regular supply of water and they must provide most things themselves. Things that cannot be made or grown on the homestead have to be brought a great distance.

Caves have a very even temperature. They stay cool in hot weather and provide warm shelter in winter.

Man-made deserts

The balance of life in arid regions is extremely delicate. It is very easily upset. Many areas that are now desert were once fertile and used in earlier times for agriculture. The changes might be caused by a number of things. The most likely reasons are changes in climate and the effect that people have upon the land.

In order to provide land to grow crops people have cleared forest areas. Especially in upland areas forests help to collect rainwater and protect the ground from rain and wind. If the land is bare the rain and wind can wash the soil away. So the slow process of forming a desert begins. It usually happens so slowly that nobody realizes what is taking place. But if there is a sudden drought or an increase in population it can happen very suddenly indeed. That is what happened in Oklahoma in the United States in the 1930's. Farmers ploughed up grazing land to grow crops. The grass that had protected the ground and held the soil together with its roots was removed. So when a drought came the soil was dried to dust and blown away by the wind. The area became known as the *Dust Bowl* and no one could farm there anymore. It took many years to reclaim the land which had been ruined by bad farming methods.

Overgrazing

If too many animals are kept on one piece of land the grass does not have time to grow again after grazing. Land that has been able to provide enough grass for a

Goats will eat practically anything. They quickly strip the land of all vegetation.

herd of cattle may no longer be able to do so. Sheep and goats are then allowed to graze the area. If they are not watched carefully they may soon turn the area into a desert. The goat particularly will eat everything in sight. Goats have been blamed for the destruction of grazing lands in the Mediterranean and parts of Persia.

Reclamation

People have always tried to make a living in the deserts of the world. It is becoming more and more important to use as much land as we can as the world's population is growing so rapidly.

The building of the Aswan dam on the Nile in Egypt has provided about 50,000 hectares of farmland.

In the United States some of the waters of the Colorado River have been directed into the Imperial Valley in Southern Colorado to water the Sonora Desert. Land which was once desert is now some of the richest farmland in the world. Desert soil is very rich in the minerals needed by plants.

In some places experiments are being carried out to try to extract the salt from seawater using atomic energy. The water can then be used to irrigate the desert. In other places the edges of deserts have been planted to try to stabilize the soil and stop it blowing away. Tree planting projects help to bind the soil and keep moisture in the air.

Farmers are being taught that it is dangerous to graze land too heavily. They are encouraged to control the size of their herds and to move them to new pastures when necessary.

Building terraces stops the top soil from being washed down the hills.

Wealth of the desert

Above: Oil is very important in many middle eastern countries. The wealth of the nation depends on it.

Below: Uranium drillers in Australia.

As there is so little rain in the desert the minerals collect on the surface of the land. In wetter climates they would be washed away. In Northern Chile a mining industry grew up based on these minerals. Large amounts of chemicals called nitrates were found. They were used for fertilizers before artificial fertilizers were developed.

Salt is another important mineral which is essential to man and animals. It is even more important in hot climates. Salt can often be collected in desert areas. In the Sahara the salt is transported by camel trains. Sometimes these camel trains are an amazing sight. On one occasion 30,000 camels were seen in one caravan.

Many other things are mined in deserts. In Australia opal mining is important. Bauxite from which aluminium is made is also found in many desert regions. Uranium is mined in the American desert and also in Australia.

Black gold

One of the most important products of the desert in recent years has been oil. It is found all through the Middle East and North Africa and also in the United States. It has brought great wealth to the countries where it has been found. However, the oil in the deserts will not last for ever and we must use it wisely.

Problems

Mining in desert areas is very difficult. The heat is very unpleasant to work in. All the food, machinery, water and anything else needed must be brought in from elsewhere, often from hundreds of miles away and at great expense.

Above: The desert in Australia is rich in minerals. But conditions are very difficult for the miners and their families.

Below: Oil pipelines in Algeria.

Books to read

Polar deserts, Wally
Herbert; Collins 1971
A closer look at deserts,
Valerie Pitt and David
Cook; Hamish Hamilton
1975
**A closer look at arctic
lands,** J.L. Hicks;
Hamish Hamilton 1976
Deserts, Margeret Tyler;
Hart-Davis 1974
Exploring Ecology, (ed)
Carole Edwards and
Cathy Kilpatrick;
Macdonald 1974
Desert animals, R. Tate;
Macdonald Educational
1971
Desert lands, Stephanie
Conell and Jennifer
Vaughan; Macdonald
Educational 1976
**Encyclopaedia of
Africa,** (ed) Keith Lye;
Macdonald Educational
1976
The desert, John
Leonard Cloudesley-
Thompson; Orbis Books
1977
**Lost World of the
Kalahari,** Laurens van
der Post; Penguin. (This
book is out of print but
your library will have a
copy.)
**Animals of tundra and
ice lands,** trans Irene
R Gibbons; Frederick
Warne 1970

Places to visit

You will find examples of
many of the birds and
animals mentioned in this
book in the zoos, wildlife
parks and bird gardens
throughout the country.
You will also find many
creatures from the dry
areas of the world which
we have mentioned.

To find a centre near your
home, consult these books
in your library:

**Wild life: A guide to
zoos, zoological
gardens and bird
gardens in the British
Isles,** K F Robins and
M A Radford; Interzoo
Publications Ltd 1974

**Wild life in Britain:
Guide to natural
habitats, safari parks
and zoos;** Automobile
Association 1976

Things to do

These are very famous
parks and zoos:

London Zoo
Regents Park
London NW1 4RY

Whipsnade Park Zoo
Dunstable
Bedfordshire

Windsor Safari Park
St Leonards
Windsor
SL4 4AY

**Woburn Wild Animal
Kingdom**
Woburn Park
Woburn
Bedfordshire

To find out more about
different desert peoples
and how they live, visit the
Museum of Mankind,
6 Burlington Gardens,
London W1

Other places to find out
more about deserts and the
plants, animals and people
that live in them are your
local museums and the
school or public library.
But also look in less
obvious places like the
supermarket. Next time
you buy a box of dates,
see where they come from.
There are also many shops
that specialise in ethnic
products often made by
desert peoples, such as
embroidered Arab dresses,
elaborate jewellery and
decorated floor and wall
coverings.

Glossary

Amphibians: Animals that spend a part of their lives on land and a part in water.

Annuals: plants that live for only one year.

Archimedes screw: a method for lifting water.

Deflation: the lifting and carrying of sand and dust by the wind.

Deposition: the laying down of sand and dust carried by the wind.

Dust Bowl: an infertile area of land created in Oklahoma as a result of over-cultivation and very dry conditions.

Herbivores: animals that only eat plants.

Integument: tough protective covering that insects have.

Invertebrates: animals that do not have a backbone.

Irrigation: watering the land by artificial means.

Marsupial: animals that have a pouch for carrying their young. The babies are born very early in their development.

Molluscs: soft-bodied animals which usually have hard shells.

Oasis: fertile spot in the desert where water is available.

Permafrost: the subsoil in polar regions. It is frozen throughout the year.

Perennial: plants which live for several years. They die back in the winter and bloom again in the spring.

Photosynthesis: Process that plants use to change energy from the sun, carbon dioxide from the air and water into food.

Quartz: a common mineral present in many rocks. It is very hard and looks glassy.

Quicksands: a mass of loose or unstable sand.

Rodents: animals such as rats, mice and squirrels. They have strong, sharp incisor teeth, but no canine teeth.

Sakia: a method for lifting water consisting of a wheel with a continuous chain of buckets.

Shaduf: a method for lifting water consisting of a pole supported on a cross bar with a bucket on one end and a weight on the other.

Sip well: the method by which the bushmen use a hollow reed to collect water from damp sand.

Wadis: a desert water course which is usually dry. When rain falls it fills very quickly and the water rushes down it in flash floods.

Index